THE GRADUATE STUDENT AS WRITER

Encouragement for the Budding Scholar

Shuyi Chua

*This book is dedicated to the graduate student
and my writing teachers.*

CONTENTS

INTRODUCTION

In 2015, I completed my Master's study and from my work for the degree, I published three journal articles from 2015-2017. Many students have asked me how I did it. Hence, I volunteered to conduct a workshop titled "Demystifying the Publication Process: A Graduate Student's Personal Experience with Writing and Publishing" at my university in 2017. This book is a development from that workshop and a consolidation of what I've learned about academic writing. It is advice given from one graduate student to another.

You might think that the best person to teach writing is one's academic advisor. However, being good at writing doesn't make one good at teaching it. Furthermore, many academic advisors do not have the time to guide their students in this important process. This is why many universities have outsourced the job of teaching students how to write to a specialized department or academic writing advisors. However, academic writing advisors may only provide generic advice, not always applicable to every student. To succeed in academia, a graduate student must take charge of his or her own writing journey and become an independent writer.

I was fortunate that during my time at the university, I was given ample opportunities to read, write and think about writing. This book is a compilation of my thoughts and ideas about academic writing and publishing. I will share what I tried, how I succeeded and what I have learned in the process. I hope that with this knowledge, writing and publishing will become less intimidating and more accessible to you. And you may be inspired to explore for yourself what works for you.

This book is intended for the graduate student of the social sciences, however, some of the advice and examples pertain to students of all fields. I've written this book in a casual tone, the way I would speak to a friend who comes to me, asking for advice. I've organized the content into short segments, each containing a practical tip or truth that you can immediately apply or ponder over. Many students have a fear of writing, owing to certain misconceptions about it. I hope to address these along the way to change the way you view writing and yourself as a writer.

To write this book, I used the same techniques in this book. I wanted to show you that it works. I started out pouring out everything I wanted to tell you about writing. Subsequently, I relied on books to support, reinforce and clarify what I had written. And while doing this, I was also re-reading and re-writing my text. At the back of my mind, I was also considering to whom to send it for review, feedback and copyediting. I hope that sharing my experience will help you find your own path.

I've divided this book into three sections – first, reflections and strategies to put you in the writer's mindset; second, a technical how-to-actually-do-it section, where you can read about the writing and publishing process that helped me; third, a section of final encouraging thoughts on the joy and art of writing and publishing. You can go straight to the section that most interests you.

SECTION ONE: REFLECTIONS AND STRATEGIES FOR THE GRADUATE STUDENT WRITER

CHAPTER 1: SEE YOUR ACADEMIC JOURNEY AS A WRITING JOURNEY

"Every artist was first an amateur."

Ralph Waldo Emerson

The graduate student is first and foremost a writer. How can this not be when what is expected of him or her are written texts - a hardbound thesis, journal articles, book chapters, assignments and the like. You might have never seen yourself as a writer before; but believe me, it helps to do so because you are going to spend a lot of time writing. To be a successful academic, you must write.

One of the key skills you should have developed by the end of your studies is the skill of writing. A skill is an acquired ability to do something. It is achieved through repetition, feedback and technique mastery. So aim to graduate not just as an expert of your field of study, but also as a trained writer, one who can commit to writing when given a task to do. Like any job, there are good and bad days; but regardless, we stick with it and get the job done. Once you have learned how to write, writing something becomes a process that you undertake; it is no longer a mystery or some form of magic (although there are always elements of these involved). You will know how to repeat that process and produce a respectable piece of text on demand.

Unlike any other job, the graduate student's primary responsibility is to become a scholar. You must remember this because there will be many distractions that threaten to take you away from writing. By writing regularly, you are paying yourself first. The skills you develop and the pieces you complete are what you take away with you into your next job and subsequent career. They are what you do for yourself.

Writing does not have to be a necessary evil, nor a chore to get through to earn a degree. Should you take some time to explore the process and rewards of scholarly writing, you will be surprised at your discoveries. You will find that being a writer is the scholar's calling. Hence, as you begin your journey as a research student, I encourage you to see yourself as a budding and amateur writer. It will change the way you approach your studies and help you value and appreciate the many opportunities to hone and practice this skill.

CHAPTER 2: USE WRITING AS A TOOL

"Writing – putting things down on paper – is what allows you to hold onto one idea while you go off and explore some idea that some small, nagging voice in the back of your mind tells you might be related to it. In and because of writing, you can discover how certain things you thought were different might turn out to have things in common; how certain things you thought were alike really turn out to be different. Writing is the mind's way of thinking beyond what it can think without an aid like paper and pen. It is also, of course, a way of reaching beyond yourself to other minds, whose only access to yours is provided by those traces of your mind you leave behind, in your writings."

Susan Horton (1982, pp. 2–3)

"I write about things I am still wrestling with, things that are important to me but that I have not yet figured out...I write to explore vexing questions and real dilemmas, to take myself into territories I have never seen before in hopes of understanding myself and the world a bit better."

Parker Palmer (1999)

Writing is an important skill for the graduate student because it is the tool for knowledge to be appraised, developed and shared. It is the way "to work out complex intellectual problems that you can't resolve in your head" (Labaree, 2012, p. 74). Therefore, writing is more than a completed product: it is a tool for thinking. Writing enables us to "put thought on trial" and prevents us from coming to a premature conclusion before we have thoroughly considered our options (Devan, 2007).

I often write to think. I find out how I view something through writing about it. To me, writing is thought put on paper. Susan Horton wrote a book called, "Thinking Through Writing" (Horton, 1982). Her book has formed the basis of my approach to writing.

Writing is a tool that can be used for recording, assessing, organizing and analyzing:

Recording: Capturing fleeting moments of inspiration (that can be more fully developed later)

Assessing: Discovering and clarifying what you know and do not know about your topic (writing helps you discover gaps in your knowledge and flaws in your reasoning)

Organizing: Structuring and sharing your thoughts and ideas in a coherent way with others (your supervisor, other scholars, etc.)

Analyzing: Consolidating and modifying all that you've read and thought about your topic (helping you see links between ideas)

It is important to grasp this concept because as an academic, you are an intellectual dealing with knowledge. You must become familiar with the most important tool for knowledge development and communication, and know how to wield it to your purposes and advantage. Without knowing how to use this tool skillfully, it is almost impossible to go far in one's academic career. Perhaps this is one of the reasons why academics are often appraised by the number of high-quality publications they publish, because they reflect how well they think as experts.

Many people think they can't write. However, if you can think it, you can write it. Writing is putting thought on paper. Unlike speaking to an audience, your readers are not there to clarify what is unclear or tell you what they want to know more about. So, you have to write in a way that is easily understandable. Oftentimes, what you are trying to convey is complex. Hence, writing involves a great deal of analytical work in deciding how best to structure your text to most effectively convey your complex thoughts to others.

CHAPTER 3: WRITE AT EVERY STAGE OF YOUR GRADUATE JOURNEY

"Hear this: You cannot begin writing early enough. And yes, I really mean it. Would that mean someone might write a first draft before venturing into the field to begin observations or interviews? Absolutely."

Harry F. Wolcott (2009, p. 18)

B ecause writing is a tool, you should begin using it to help you as early as possible. Use writing to help you discover how you think about things. We do not need to wait until our thoughts are all formed before we begin writing. Begin wherever you are as these early thoughts will be the fodder for the grander thoughts that come later.

Use writing early on to help you explore possible threads or ideas that can introduce a topic. Use it to record information about the methods you use or thoughts you don't want to forget.

Don't have an idea how to organize your findings? Draw a mind-map or write them out in prose. Even if they do not end up in your thesis, they will have served as the impetus for subsequent thoughts. Some of these passages may even end up as parts of your assignments, journal articles or final thesis.

Read something impactful? Use writing to comment about it. An author's writings are his or her intellectual output. Your comments on those writings are *your* intellectual output. It is not that difficult to be original. As for me, I keep a blog; and every time I am inspired by something I have read or a thought or an idea, I blog about it. This way, I am consistently leaving a record of something I find meaningful and useful that will be searchable in a time to come.

These initial writings or scribbles also serve as material for discussion with your advisors and peers. Some of us are not sure what to speak to our advisors about, and these writings will provide a way to look at how you thought about an issue at a certain point in time, so you can get comments. Writing is thought externalized.

CHAPTER 4: THE FIRST JOURNAL ARTICLE IS THE HARDEST

I f you have never written a complete journal article, I must warn you that your first one is often the hardest. Like a stream of water tunneling its way through the ground, the first time always requires the most effort. With more time and tries, as the path downstream becomes carved out, the water will flow with greater and greater ease.

My advisor was the person who first encouraged me in the craft of writing. Prior to working with her, I had never written a full draft of an article. And writing my first one was not easy. Early in my data collection, my advisor asked me to write a draft for a journal, which I did. To my dismay, she was disappointed with what I had produced. It was filled with red markings and she told me that she had wanted to tear it up when she first read it. She told me to redo it.

This was difficult feedback to take. I was devastated and did not know what to do next. If you find yourself in a similar situation, know that it is completely normal for a beginning writer to experience challenges in finding his or her written voice and presenting ideas in an acceptable manner to the scholarly community. Do not be discouraged should your early work be heavily criticized. And do not give up. This is normal and common among all writers – novice, expert, amateur and professional.

I continued working on that article and my advisor and I submitted it to the editor. After a few months, I received the reviewers' comments and was displeased that it was accepted with major revisions. The comments were difficult to take, and I took a while to regain my composure and squarely face the new task of heavily editing the work to make it ready for publication. (I later learned that this verdict was much better than being rejected because when you use the feedback given to improve your work, the chances of being published in that journal become high, since they had already invested so much time and effort in your work.)

As I proceeded to work on it, I was fortunate to have a friend who was doing his PhD in political science at the time, and I consulted him on making some of the changes. I still remember that day when he sat down with me in the Singapore Botanic Gardens to go through my article line by line, helping me to more accurately convey what I had wanted to say. His kindness at lending his mind to help me with my work has stayed with me. It is hard for me now to reject someone, who comes to me needing help with his or her writing.

The experience also taught me that writing is a painstaking process that involves clarifying again and again what I am thinking and how best to communicate it through words. There are no short cuts. It also taught me that help comes from many places, not necessarily your advisor; and if we ask for help, we will find it.

The article was finally accepted and the next shock came when it was returned to me copyedited. I knew that grammar wasn't my strength, but to see the whole article covered in red tracking shook me. Since then, I have engaged a professional copyeditor to clean up my articles before I submit them.

I am happy to say that once I experienced this first publication, the subsequent ones became easier and easier, as there were fewer new things to expect of the writing process. In this book, I am sharing with you what I know of the writing process and other lessons I've learned along the way.

CHAPTER 5:
DIFFERENT OUTLETS
OF PUBLICATIONS

"People have to have outlets for what may not yet be useful. They need situations in which they can try out and sharpen their skills. So be persistent, try out and sharpen yours!"
David R. Krathwohl (1994, p. 30)

Once you see yourself as a budding writer, you will not see written assignments in the same way. Each opportunity to write is an opportunity to hone your skills. And each assignment has the potential to develop into something publishable. If not, each paragraph has the potential to be reworked into something for another assignment or piece further downstream in the writing process. As emerging writers, we must value any opportunity to write, even if it doesn't seem to be a high-impact one.

The type of writing of most value to an academic is the peer-reviewed journal and there are many types, each with a different value assigned to it, depending on its tier. These are the most coveted outlets that every academic vies for as these determine ranking and reputation in many universities. As a beginner, it is good to know that these higher-stake publications are not the only outlets for writing. (Note: the high-impact factor should not be the ultimate goal of an academic but the production of high-quality work.)

It may make more sense to gain some experience by writing for lower-stake publications or outlets, in which it is easier to get published, to practice the skill of communicating to a community of scholars. These outlets include online journals, book chapters, conference proceedings, book reviews and editorials. These days, most of us search online for the material we need. I believe that as long as a high-quality article is searchable online and reaches its intended audience to be read and cited, it is a good enough place to begin.

I am going to put some emphasis on book reviews because I find them an underrated but great exercise in learning how to read and critique someone else's work.

Book Review

> *"Book reviews are an underappreciated art form in academic writing. Read them. Write them. Pay no heed to anyone who insists that book reviews – whether published or electronic – "don't count" as scholarly contributions. Anything that makes you a more astute writer/editor contributes immensely to your ability."*
> *Harry F. Wolcott (2009, p. 108)*

The book review is an opportunity for you to get a taste of academic writing and publishing. The experience of writing for a large audience is different from writing for your advisor. For one, you become more aware that your audience consists of "real people." It alerts you to the responsibility of publishing. Being aware of your readership changes your relationship to the text you produce. You begin to have a sense of how you fit into the larger community of scholars. Commenting publicly on the work of another scholar, establishes you as an expert in the same field. You become the scholar you are intended to be.

I remember the first time I was asked to review a book. The book editor of a journal, who I met through a conference, emailed me to ask if I would be interested in reviewing a book related to my area of study. I was shocked and honored at being given that opportunity, but was also in doubt about my capability to review a history book, not being trained in history. To add to my concern, the author of the book was a friend. I did not want to offend him in any way.

I decided to embrace the learning opportunity, in spite of my doubts. Once I received the book, I proceeded to study it carefully, reading it at least two times. I consulted my writing buddy about the book review and she shared that we are rarely taught how to read a book. I agreed with her. I was determined that for the sake of my academic reputation, I must do a good first job, so I took learning how to read seriously with the help of a book called, "How to Read a Book" (Adler & Van Doren, 2014). I turned to the chapter on how to read history and learned what is expected of a good history book. I then completed the book review and it was published in a reputable journal (Chua, 2016).

The second opportunity to write a book review was self-initiated. My advisor, the book review editor of a journal, had asked if there was any book I wanted to review. And yes, there was one. There was a newly-published philosophical treatise on patriotism that I wanted to read. She proceeded to contact the publisher, and soon I had a copy of the book. I read this book 5-6 times as I was new to philosophy as a genre, and I was not naturally inclined toward it. So yes, I also relied on "How to Read a Book" to learn how to read philosophy (Adler & Van Doren, 2014). This book review was published (Chua, 2017a).

Prior to writing these two book reviews, I had never read a history or a philosophy book from beginning to end. But after this experience, I was more open to books of different genres. I realized that I was capable of transcending genres. I started to appreciate how reading works of scholars from fields and backgrounds different from my own has enriched my understanding of my topic in a way that could not have happened had I stuck to familiar works.

How do you get such an opportunity? If you have a colleague who is a book review editor of a journal, tell him or her that you have interest in reviewing books on certain topics. Many book reviews editors are given books by publishers; they pile up on their desks waiting for someone to come along and take them. If you offer to do a review, you are assured a chance to see your name in print.

Editorial

Editorials are another type of writing you can do. In your university, there may be newsletters or magazines seeking writers. I was given a chance to write an editorial to be emailed to the university's mailing list, including alumni and business partners. One of my lecturers was asked if he wanted to write an editorial piece on national education, my pet topic; but because he did not specialize in this area but knew I did, he forwarded the email and asked if I would like to do it instead.

I jumped at the opportunity because I wanted to share my research with a non-academic audience. Ironically, in my university, we do not talk much about "popular writing" or writing intended for non-scholars such as the everyday person. In science, it is known as science communication, and this ability is highly prized when you know how to communicate simply and with impact to laypeople. I value this type of non-academic communication because much of what we do as scholars never reaches the masses except through such forms of writing. To be able to communicate simply the complex ideas we deal with daily is also demonstrative of our understanding of our subject.

Another thing I enjoyed about writing this piece was that I could incorporate my opinions freely and openly. As opposed to research articles that require verifiable evidence, writing this editorial allowed me to use anecdotes from personal experience. I decided to write about how technology has changed the way teachers teach citizenship in schools (Chua, 2017b).

Completing this piece of writing was not easy and additional work on top of my other responsibilities as a graduate student. The editor of this piece had many expectations and I had to make many drafts before I gained her approval. But I saw this as valuable experience in my journey of being a writer generally, and not just as an academic.

Conference Proceeding

Another important outlet for publishing are conference proceedings. Conference proceedings are a published record of conference presentations. Not all conferences require you to submit an article prior to your attendance. Some require a proposal and others just an abstract. Whatever written text is required, you will need to prepare an oral presentation.

I encourage you to attend as many of these reputable conferences as possible to give these oral presentations. Here are the reasons why:

1. You get to meet and mingle with other academics studying in similar fields. Through learning about their work and sharing yours, knowledge is exchanged. You may even make some friends, like I have, that last beyond academia!

2. You get to travel around the world! Do take advantage of this. One of the best gifts we can give ourselves as writers is our own personal development. The more we experience and know about the world, the greater the depth of insight in our thinking and writing.

3. You get the opportunity and motivation to write. Whether or not the conference asks for more than just an abstract, you control how much effort to put into it. You may decide to write a conference article and then turn it into a journal article as I will elaborate on in the next section.

4. You can cite your conference presentation. Not all research is eventually published as journal articles. But as you write, you may be required to cite some of the findings merely mentioned in conferences. By regularly updating the audience on your research progress through

regular conference attendance, you leave a trail for others to follow. This is why this is my favorite mode of publication: conference presentations are much easier to prepare compared to journal articles, yet they are still deemed as citable sources of information by the scholarly community. They are perfect for the budding scholar!

While working as a research associate at my institute, I aimed to attend one international conference a year. Because of these conferences, I've traveled to Siem Reap, Cambodia; Seoul, Korea; Beijing, China and Birmingham, UK. I have also had the experience of organizing a conference in Singapore, attended by some of the colleagues I had met at conferences. I am lucky that I was able to find funding for most of these conferences, except one in New Orleans, USA.

I found it worthwhile, however, to pay for my attendance at the conference in New Orleans, because I was trying out a new methodology called Q-Methodology, and I had a lot of questions. It turned out to be a good idea as one of the professors I met personally sat down with me at this conference and taught me how to use a computer program to analyze my results. I also learned about the potential and applications of Q-methodology through listening to other presentations. So, depending on how you make the best of each conference, you can reap manifold benefits!

Do not have enough money? Use your ingenuity to find funds. A friend of mine emailed the organizers of a conference to ask if she could volunteer for them in exchange for a waived conference fee, and they agreed. She found a good way to get around the expensive conference fee.

CHAPTER 6: EACH CONFERENCE PRESENTATION = ONE JOURNAL ARTICLE

B ecause we have limited time and energy as graduate students, it is important to find creative ways to streamline the writing and publishing process. This could mean viewing each task given to you for its potential of developing into a journal article or a section of your thesis.

Since we are already investing time and effort to produce a piece of intellectual work, why not just invest a little more and convert it into something of value beyond the initial effort? Having some kind of strategy or plan for publishing will help you put in less effort and gain more in the long run.

One of the best ways to do this is to convert a conference presentation into a journal article. Let me share how I did it.

1. Sign up for a conference, ready with your abstract.
2. Based on this abstract, start writing your article.
3. Use this working document to help you prepare your

slides nearer the presentation date.

4. Volunteer to give a presentation to your advisors, colleagues or fellow graduate students as practice for the conference and be attentive to their feedback.
5. Use that feedback to improve and shape both your article and slides.
6. Give your presentation at the conference and collect a second round of feedback.
7. Make use of this feedback to refine your article.
8. Your article is ready for submission!

This process is excellent because you are tapping into an external source to motivate you to write. It is like signing up for a competition first and then training for it. The various deadlines of the conference will motivate you to keep working on the task. In addition, one of the things most important for producing good writing is having feedback and knowing how your listeners and readers (the community of scholars) are responding to what you say. With this approach, rather than fearing the comments and questions that arise during your presentation, you will eagerly anticipate them because they are exactly what you need to improve your work. Oftentimes, your audience will give you fresh perspectives that can help you sharpen your arguments.

Additionally, a conference presentation is ideal for transformation into an accompanying journal article because of its scope and size. Unlike a bulky thesis where you have to think hard about dividing it into appropriately-sized sections for a journal article, the conference presentation is already packaged in an appropriate size and form. It will be a beautiful timestamp of your thoughts and ideas about your topic at a point in time. Yes, that is all it is. Don't let the thought that your views on an issue will change with time or are not yet at their best stop you from writing and publishing earlier.

My second publication, "Rethinking Critical Patriotism: A Case of Constructive Patriotism in Social Studies Teachers in Singapore" was the result of using this method (Chua & Sim, 2017). In fact, when I attended the conference, I already had a draft in hand, and was able to edit it immediately, after my session. By the end of the conference, I was ready to submit the article.

There are variations to this method. More recently, I had written to a professor at my university who oversees an online journal. I shared with him the abstract of my conference presentation and asked if he might be interested in having an article like it in his journal. I was willing to turn it into an article just for his journal. And guess what? He said, "Yes!" And the result was the article, "Storytelling in the Social Studies Classroom."

There is a story behind "Storytelling in the Social Studies Classroom." It was the product of a research proposal I eventually rejected for my PhD study. I wrote a proposal for the initial study, literature review complete and all, but I decided not to pursue it. Rather than wasting that proposal, I thought to myself, why not try to publish it somewhere. I had always desired to be the sole author of my work and always wanted to write for practitioners. I wanted to write in an enjoyable manner for non-academic so this was my chance! And that's what I did.

CHAPTER 7: WHY PUBLISH?

My advisor phoned me to let me know that our first article together had been accepted, and she was happy and wanted to celebrate it. Rather than feeling happy at that news, I was horrified that my "lousy piece of work" was now available for the world to read. At that time, I was new to my field of study. I was trained as a biologist, so what did I know about education or citizenship? Also, I was not confident about my ability to write.

I've grown past that stage. People talk a lot about graduate students having the imposter syndrome, which I had too. It is the feeling that what you have produced is a fluke and not borne out of true scholarship. What I have learned over the years is to be fair to myself. Yes, the work is not perfect, and that's fine. It's not totally bad either and has some intellectual contribution to make. Publishing tells me that I am, at the very least, potentially contributing in some way to someone's thinking about something.

When we embark on our studies, we are seeking answers to questions of importance to others and ourselves. We interpret, analyze and report our findings. And then we communicate them to the community. Thereafter, others can continue or debate the work. Publishing is a way to ensure that this knowledge has a wide and lasting impact. Whatever you say at a conference or write for an assignment will not last, no matter how intelligent or impactful it is. Once the conference is over or the semester moves on, no one will remember what you had said or written. But what you publish will last, always there for someone to search, find and read. You leave a mark that will continue to make an impact long after you have moved on in your career or die. Collectively, through publishing, we ensure that knowledge advances.

CHAPTER 8: START SMALL WHERE YOU ARE

"Maybe it takes a certain amount of practice; maybe it means exploring lots of avenues before finding the one that leads the way to a real contribution. Legislators complain about the wasted research funds that result in useless publications that don't make a difference. Would we have the research that really does make a difference without the other?"

David R. Krathwohl (1994, p. 30)

Some of us hesitate to publish until we are certain what we have to say will be impactful. One of my professors once told me that it's better to publish one impactful article than many non-impactful ones. The more I thought about what he said, the less realistic it seemed for any graduate student. It might work for someone who has established a career but definitely not for someone like you and me, who are just beginning ours.

If this is the reason you have delayed writing and publishing, think about it. To finally arrive at that one impactful article, you need some practice in writing and publishing non-impactful ones. If you wait until you have finally conceptualized that grand theory or idea, when you want to publish it, you might find that you don't have the associated skills to write it up, find the right journal and pitch it to the right audience, etc. These are the skills you need to practice, so you will always be ready to produce high quality and rigorous work.

You can always see these smaller "less impactful" strands of research, as part of the massive project you are undertaking. Meaning, at the end of 10 years of publishing less impactful articles, you can put them all together into a grand theory, or even a book! So it is not a waste. It's about seeing things long term. We have to make the best of the system and tools available to us. Practice now and reap the rewards later. Have that grand goal in mind, but take small, practical steps towards it.

Moreover, whether a work is impactful or non-impactful is subjective. Something impactful to one reader may not be to another. Something impactful today may no longer be so tomorrow. Do not let your uncertainty over whether your work will make a difference stop you from writing and publishing. We cannot know for sure the impact our words will have until they are written and read.

CHAPTER 9: THE BEST TIME TO PUBLISH

You may already suspect that my orientation on this issue based on my advice about turning conference presentations into journal articles. I believe that every student should begin publishing before they graduate! Why? The best time to learn how to write is while in the university, as you have access to an advisor, lecturers, fellow graduate students, and all the resources offered to you, including an academic writing staff. And do not think that you don't have the material to publish. Your literature review, if done well, is a potential segment for publication. You don't even have to have results yet to publish.

Some of us think that publishing is only for the very smart. But, actually, it is for the most persevering. To publish, you need to be hardworking to write drafts and humble in approaching others for help when needed. You will want to tap into minds more intelligent than your own. Where can you find all these experts? You will find them in your own university, among colleagues and classmates or at conferences where all the brightest minds on your topic gather. It is important to find support outside the university. The going can get tough and help, in any form from anyone, is wonderful. If you can access this stream of intelligence, not only by reading academic works but also through interacting with the professors who write them, you will more likely produce high-quality work.

Another reason why I encourage publishing early is that it gives you credibility when you finally defend your thesis. When you cite your peer-reviewed publications, mention them with pride. They imply that your work has already undergone a thorough evaluation by other scholars. This puts examiners at ease, as they know that you have already been examined by the community and found satisfactory.

CHAPTER 10:
USE BOOKS AS RESOURCES AND FOR ENCOURAGEMENT

"All that mankind has done, thought, gained or been: it is lying as in magic preservation in the pages of books."

Thomas Carlyle

My friend and now PhD student, Nicholas, taught me how to use how-to-write books. One day, I was frustrated about my writing progress and visited his office; he introduced me to two books on writing – "How to Write and Publish a Scientific Paper" (Gastel & Day, 2006) and "A Short Guide to Writing about Biology" (Pechenik, 2015). He used these books to help him with his own writing and told me I could search for the Social Science version of the second book, which I did find: *"A Short Guide to Writing about Social Science" (Cuba, 2002)*.

This was my first introduction to books that teach how to

write; and since then, I have fallen for this genre of literature. I discovered that through these books, I have access to the world's best writing teachers. Subsequently, I have also discovered writing teachers on Masterclass (Masterclass, 2018). Malcolm Gladwell and Bob Woodward teach lessons that are particularly helpful for non-fiction writing. Fiction writers, many of whom are on Masterclass, also have much to teach us. It is rather fun to learn from these expert writers.

Sometimes, I refer to my "teachers" when I am stuck at a certain section of writing and am not sure what to include. At other times when I lack motivation, prior to writing, I read a passage from one of these books or watch a video clip on Masterclass, and they serve as inspiration for the writing to come.

Over time, I accumulated a list of my favorite go-to books for writing help. Very often, more than providing practical help, they encourage and inspire you by including advice and inspiration from their own observations and life with regards to writing.

The following books are my favorites by topic:

Understanding the whole writing process:
- Becker, H. S. (2007). *Writing for social scientists: How to start and finish your thesis, book, or article* (2 ed.) Chicago, IL: The University of Chicago Press.
- Wolcott, H. F. (2009). *Writing up qualitative research* (3 ed.) Thousand Oaks, CA: SAGE Publications, Inc.
- Elbow, P. (1998). *Writing without teachers*. New York, NY: Oxford University Press.
- Single, P. B. (2009). *Demystifying dissertation writing: A streamlined process from choice of topic to final text*. Stirling, VI: Stylus Publishing, LLC.
- Horton, S. R. (1900). *Thinking through writing*. Baltimore, ML: Johns Hopkins
- Kamler, B. and Thomson, P. (2014) Helping doctoral

students write: Pedagogies for supervision (2 ed.) Florence, KY: Routledge

- Williams, V. K. (2016) I am ~~not~~ a writer... and I am ~~just~~ in graduate school: A guide to writing critically, clearly and coherently. Tampa, FL: Chrysalis Consulting LLC

Effective week-by-week guide to produce a journal article:

- Belcher, W. L. (2009). *Writing your journal article in 12 weeks: A guide to academic publishing success.* Los Angeles, CA: SAGE

Improving technique and style:

- Brogan, J. A. (1973). Clear technical writing. New York, NY: McGraw-Hill Book Company
- Williams, J. M. & Bizup, J. (2016). *Style: Lessons in clarity and grace* (12 ed.). Boston, MA: Pearson
- Perry, C. R. (2011). *The fine art of technical writing: Key points to help you think your way through writing scientific or technical publications, theses, term papers, & business reports.* Scotts Valley, CA: CreateSpace Independent Publishing Platform.
- Strunk, W. & White, E. B. (2007). *The elements of style.* 4th ed. Boston, MA: Pearson

Topical on different aspects of academic writing:

- Cuba, L. (2002). *A short guide to writing about social science* (4 ed.). New York, NY: Longman
- Gastel, B. & Day, R. A. (2016). *How to write and publish a scientific paper* (8 ed.). Santa Barbara, CA: Greenwood.
- Packer, N. H. & Timpane, J. (1986). *Writing worth reading: A practical guide.* New York, NY: St. Martin's Press.
- Rawlin, J. & Metzger, S. (2009) The writer's way. (7 ed.) Boston, MA: Houghton Mifflin Company

Books on writing by fiction writers

- Bird by Bird by Anne Lamott

- The Writing Life by Anne Dillard

SECTION TWO: THE WRITING PROCESS SIMPLIFIED

CHAPTER 11: THE OVERALL PICTURE

"Almost all good writing begins with terrible first efforts. You need to start somewhere. Start by getting something – anything – down on paper. A friend of mine says that the first draft is the down draft – you just get it down. The second draft is the up draft – you fix it up. You try to say what you have to say more accurately. And the third draft is the dental draft, where you check every tooth, to see if it's loose or cramped or decayed, or even, God help us, healthy."

Anne Lamott (1994, pp. 25–26)

What does academic writing and publishing entail? As I was thinking about it, preparing for my workshop, I realized that the writing process reflects the publication process. There are four steps: Drafting/Writing, Feedback, Rewriting and Editing/Copyediting. The difference is that you are the one directing the process during writing; but during publishing, others are more involved.

The writing process reflects the publication process

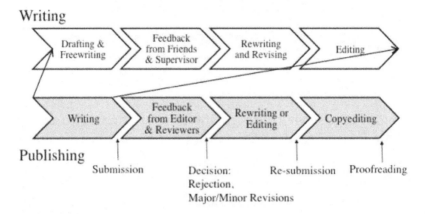

Writing

Publishing

CHAPTER 12: DRAFTING

"There is no such thing as good writing, only good rewriting."

Robert Graves

"The moment you generate sentences that might appear in your completed account, you have begun your writing. Whether your earliest efforts survive your subsequent pruning and editing is quite another matter and not of consequence at this point."

Harry F. Wolcott (2009, p. 9)

The most important word you must become accustomed to is – "draft". A draft is a preliminary version of a piece of writing. There are many versions of drafts. Lamott (1994) calls the first ones "shitty first drafts." And the more drafts you go through, the closer you get to the final version worthy of submission. The process will always work this way. You begin with a rough idea of what you want to say. And then through repeated editing and updating, you clarify and refine it. In the end, you produce a piece of writing that more or less captures what you had wanted to say at that point in time.

People may be intimidated by the idea of writing because they only see the final version produced by others and compare it to their own first draft, not knowing that the best works once began as "shitty first drafts." One of my favorite quotations on writing is from Barbara Williams: "Writing is only 1% vision and 99% revision." I had printed out and pasted this truth on my table throughout my academic journey as a constant reminder that it doesn't take brilliance to write. It takes producing a shitty first draft and then the patience and hard work to turn it into a final draft.

Drafting is a complex process where you begin combining what others have said about the topic at hand (through referencing and citing) with what you, yourself, have to say about that issue (your own voice). Learning to tell the difference between what others think and what you think, and the nuances of each, are skills vital to good academic writing. At this stage, it may not be that important to get the details down pat.

CHAPTER 13: FREEWRITING

"The reason not to perfect a work as it progresses is that, concomitantly, original work fashions a form the true shape of which it discovers only as it proceeds, so the early strokes are useless, however fine their sheen. Only when a paragraph's role in the context of the whole work is clear can the envisioning writer direct its complexity of detail to strengthen the work's end."

Annie Dillard (1990)

Related to drafting is the concept of freewriting (Elbow, 1998). Freewriting means allowing yourself to follow your train of thought through written words, even if they are not yet coherent, elegant or make total sense. You are not stopping your thoughts in their tracks by correcting them before they have reached their endpoints. So rather than throwing away ideas that do not work, leave them where they are because they might lead to other more-fitting thoughts. We can return later and remove the old thoughts if they are not relevant. If we continuously stop our thoughts in their tracks, we hinder their natural flow.

Not everybody will enjoy freewriting. Wolcott (2009) says there are two types of writers – bleeders and freewriters. You may be the bleeder. You conceptualize your argument from top to bottom and then write your article. If that is your idea of what writing involves and you hate it, freewriting is an alternative that may work for you. Discovering that I was a freewriter and doing more and more freewriting has helped me produce vast amounts of texts and drafts quickly, which has become my strategy in writing. I write a lot at first and edit a lot later.

If writing has never been your cup of tea, I strongly advise giving freewriting a try and see how freely and abundantly you will naturally produce thoughts and texts. Once you let go of the idea that producing text is difficult and must be perfect, you will have overcome a big hurdle, preventing you from becoming a writer. You will begin to see how writing is a tool to process your own thinking about an issue.

CHAPTER 14: REWRITING

"You can write first drafts quickly and carelessly exactly because you know you will be critical later."

Howard S. Becker (2008, p. 89)

W e can afford to be this extravagant with our words and let our thoughts flow freely only because in the next stage, we will be rewriting whatever we have penned. Rewriting or editing is the process whereby we read through what we have written to see if it is coherent and says what we meant to say. When you're ready for this stage, you should already have your working draft out. And now, this draft is about to be heavily edited.

Drafting is hard work, and so is rewriting. You have allowed your thoughts and ideas to flow freely during drafting; but, now, you need to be more disciplined and put the pieces together in a logical form that is coherent and clear. You will need to select what is good, shelve what may not be relevant at this point in time and delete what is bad. Rewriting may require a major re-structuring of your article, entailing ways to reduce repetition and redundancies of what you have written. It may also require deciding what knowledge the reader needs to understand what you are saying or what to eliminate that the reader likely knows.

If you have become proficient in drafting and freewriting, you will notice that the difficulty is no longer in producing text but in deleting text to make way for more appropriate material. I wrote this reflection early on in the rewriting process of my first journal article, *"The difficulty with writing is not that I do not have enough ideas but that I have too many, and I have to learn to pick and choose only those that I can thread together into a beautiful necklace. This often involves abandoning some of my favorite beads that do not fit the theme of the necklace I'm stringing together. - May 5 2014*

Rewriting can be painful when you're new to it, especially if it's your first draft and the first time you have produced so much text. But it is important that we learn to be "ruthless" and say, "that can go." Essential to re-writing is not to overly identify with what you have written but have the heart to shelve any ideas and sentences that do not fit at the moment. Writing is hard work, and so we often overvalue what we have written. Yet, what I have found for myself is that the fastest way to write is to be quick in doing a draft and then heartless enough to remove what does not fit, so that something better can take its place. Be willing to throw away the entire beginning of a work.

CHAPTER 15: FEEDBACK

"We all run the risk of getting tunnel vision when writing up our own research, failing to see the broader implications for remaining unaware of relevant work that might provide a fresh or clearer perspective."

Harry F. Wolcott (2009, p. 73)

Feedback is a powerful tool that gives you access to an individual's expertise, resources, intelligence and perspectives. Feedback can challenge what you previously thought was true, point you to ideas you have never considered, spot errors in your reasoning and identify gaps in your writing. The more tried and tested and criticism-proof your work is, the higher the chance it will be accepted for publication: because there is less for reviewers to pick on.

As you rewrite, feedback is one of the most helpful tools you will need. A reader can give you fresh perspectives and help you see your work from a fresh angle. I am fortunate to have a writing buddy, Mala. We write and give each other feedback. If you look at the acknowledgement sections of my three published articles,

I always include the person who gave me the most vital feedback and helped shape the direction and outcome of the article. I would never submit an article for review unless and until one of my trusted scholarly friends has taken a good, hard look at it. Without the help of friends, my work would never be as good as it could be.

May you offer to play this role for other graduate students in exchange for them for doing the same for you. As a reviewer, it is important to be gentle when giving critical feedback. It is important to note that most of us are new to criticisms of our work. And many of us value our ideas so highly that we may be disappointed at any negative feedback. As a recipient of feedback, we must learn to be grateful, whatever form that feedback takes, that someone took the time to carefully read our work and to give us his or her honest opinions. We also need not heed every advice given to us. We are still in charge!

If we have the right attitude – not being afraid to ask for feedback and we are humble enough to consider what others say and whether we agree with them, I assure you that the rate of improvement in our writing will be much faster than if we had simply relied on your own mind for critical feedback. We all have blind spots, and most of us are immune to our errors of thought because we only write what we believe in.

CHAPTER 16: FEAR OF FEEDBACK

"Writing is an art. Initially, I approach it with my own bare hands, molding and restructuring it into shape. Towards its completion, I come with a chisel, chipping off bits and pieces to reveal the sculpture. My work has a frame - the word limit. And like an artist, I have put in so much tears, sweat and blood into my work that any criticism is hard to bear."

7 September 2014

Have you heard how artists invest themselves in their art such that their art becomes their identity? Many do not take criticism well. I suggest to you that as a writer, you are also an artist. You are expressing yourself creatively through academic writing. Thus, if you ever feel afraid of sharing your work, it is normal.

Many people do not dare ask for feedback and are afraid to share their work. This is not surprising as writing is a deeply emotional labor. For many of us, writing comes from a place deep within us and we are afraid to be criticized because it affects how we think of ourselves.

Given this reality, to be successful in academic writing, we may need to separate ourselves from our work and see the two as independent. You have a true self that is ever learning and evolving, and you have pieces of writing that only reflect your thoughts at a particular point in time.

When I first received the email from the editor telling me about the comments two reviewers had made about my first article, I remember feeling so discouraged that I didn't dare read the feedback for a few days. Thankfully, my writing buddy encouraged me, and I swallowed my pride and embarrassment and continued working on that piece of work. It was later on well received.

Writing requires courage. You cannot be sure how your readers and reviewers will receive your work, and it's highly likely that they may not like what you had to say or how you said it. However, still say it loud and clear: Do not let your fear of criticism stop you from expressing what you believe to be true at a point in time. If later, someone gives you feedback, causing you to rethink what you believe, it is good and important to your development as a writer and human being. Writing requires courage because you may very well know that your work is not perfect, and may never be, yet you still put it out there for all the world to read.

May I suggest to you that it is perfectly fine to put your thoughts and ideas out there even though they are not quite perfect. Because you, as you are today, are doing the work, not the writer you desire to be 10 years later. Yes, who you are today is all you have. You don't have all the time, help and resources in the world to produce what you are writing. There will always be a gap between what you can currently and potentially do. And, more importantly, the only way you can become a better writer is by writing and allowing what you have written to be read – allowing your ideas to interact with the world and find a new equilibrium.

One of my favorite quotations is from Aristotle – "For the things we have to learn before we can do them, we learn by doing them."

This is one of the ironies in life. We wish we could read all the textbooks on writing and hope that by doing so, we will write well. However, it's not enough to think about writing; writing skills can only be developed through writing.

What this means is that we must not be afraid to start, continue and complete a work. Then allow this work to be appraised by others, whether our reviewers or readers. If we hold the idea that we must first meet a certain standard before we can start, we forfeit the experience of learning through the process. Thus, we must not be afraid to make mistakes – and make many of them – or to produce substandard work, for this is the way to master something.

Have you ever noticed that some published books have many editions? Even established authors spot errors in their work and change the way they think about issues over time. This is why there is a need to update one's work with time. We are no different from the greats.

CHAPTER 17: EDITING

"The unnecessary words take up room and are thus uneconomic. They cheat, demanding attention by hinting at profundities and sophistication they don't contain. Seeming to mean something, those extra words mislead readers about what is being said."

Howard S. Becker (2008, p. 79)

"The aim of writing is to convey thoughts and information as clearly as possible, without superfluous words and cumbersome expressions."

Daphne HP Ng

Editing, the last stage of the writing process, has to do with refining and perfecting your work. If drafting and rewriting are the heavy construction and renovation work, respectively, editing is the laying down of decorative touches and the cleaning up of the house, before it is presented to guests. Polishing your work and making it clear and easy to read is being respectful to your reader.

Additionally, the fewer words used to bring your points across, the greater their impact. This step involves the removal of "superfluous information", known as "noise", which contributes to a lack of clarity (Brogan, 1973, p. xi). If you are looking to do this well, "Clear Technical Writing" is an amazing text with many effective exercises (Brogan, 1973). I am not sure why it is out-of-print, frankly! Let me quote from the book's preface:

"Though it overloads their sentences, and burdens and mis-guides their readers, most writers do not know they are creating semantic noise. The purpose of this text is to help you become aware of noise sources. For example, you will learn to remove simple repetitions of meaning, such as "We are *actively* testing"; overly heavy words, such as "It *exists*," rather than "It *is*"; and ponderous expressions: "We made a *measurement*," when "We *measured*" would do." (Brogan, 1973, p. xii)

Not to mention that in the writing and publishing industry, word count matters. We have limited space for printing and limited attention spans for reading. Initially, you may find that producing text is difficult, but the better you become at drafting and editing, the more you will find that the real problem is reducing the amount of text and saying all you want to say in as few words as possible.

This is the part where you read your writing a few times over and make minor tweaks before you send it out. It is important to give yourself sufficient time to edit your work and see that this last stage is also an important part of academic writing.

CHAPTER 18: COOL-DOWN PERIOD

"Like any break, cool-down refreshes you. Then, once refreshed, you can step back from what you've been working on to truly see it. You know what should be there, but is it really there? You know what you meant to say, but did you really say it? The perspective you gain from cooling down will help you spot and correct faults in the logic flow, trim unnecessary words, and invigorate flabby text."

Carol Perry (2011, p. 75)

T he final stages of editing and copyediting would be enhanced if you include a cooling down period. As graduate students, we are so used to working hard that we forget the value of rest. Even when not working, things are progressing, because our subconscious continues to be active. This is obvious when we allow a cooling down period for a piece of work.

Perry (2011) wrote, "Distancing yourself physically from your creation allows you to disengage from it mentally. And by disengaging, you effectively separate the writing stage from the editing stage - that is, the stage in which you scrutinize and revise what you've composed. Naturally, you're always doing some editing while composing. But much of that will have been done piece-meal, without an adequate overview (p. 75)."

Do not feel guilty when you need a break. Be willing to take one so you can take advantage of a rested and sharpened mind to have a more critical look at your work. Go and do something you enjoy!

And, dear graduate student, please always practice self-care! It is not worth it to lose your mental, emotional and/or physical well-ness over your studies. There is more to life than completing your studies and earning a degree. The graduate journey is a long one, and finding a sustainable way to last the journey is the key.

CHAPTER 19: COPYEDITING

"That academic writers make little use of freelance editors can be attributed, I believe, to frugality and a lack of precedent. There is no shortage of professional help available. We seem willing to invest great amounts of time at writing, and considerable sums on having the latest hardware and software available, yet nary a cent for editing."

Harry F. Wolcott (2009, p. 112)

Some of us are not native speakers of English. Some of us are, but grammar and attention to details are not our strength. If so, consider sending your work to a friend who is stronger in this regard. Get help in cleaning up the language before final submission. This is a great confidence booster and ensures that poor language is not one of the reasons why you are rejected. Reading corrections made by a friend also helps you learn to improve your writing overall.

If you do not want to trouble a friend and if you can afford it, consider paying for the services of a professional copyeditor. For example, for this book, I found a copyeditor on Upwork. I posted a job, including my expectations, and many freelancers responded with interest! I chose a copyeditor who charges within my budget and whose profile I found suitable. It may take some trial and error to find a good fit, but this is definitely something to consider. Never let poor language become an excuse not to write or publish. It's your thoughts and ideas that count!

SECTION THREE:
THE JOY AND ART
OF WRITING

CHAPTER 20: WRITING AN ARTICLE WORTH READING

"The writer's object is - or should be - to hold the reader's attention. I want the reader to turn the page and keep on turning to the end. This is accomplished only when the narrative moves steadily ahead, not when it comes to a weary standstill, overloaded with every item uncovered in the research."

Barbara Tuchman (Pace, 1989)

Writing pieces of academic works that keeps the reader eager to turn the pages is what I aspire to as a writer. I keep this at the back of my mind as I write. I choose to write about things that amaze and excite me. One of my favorite compliments is when the reader tells me that he or she has enjoyed my work. Reading is hard work; and it is my pleasure that I have made it worth someone's while.

Academic pieces have a poor reputation in terms of ease of reading. When I come across a well-written article, I am often amazed and want to read it again and again. I do have favorite articles.

I think that as scholars, one gift we can give our readers besides knowledge is an enjoyable time! This emphasizes the fact that the writer is more than a knowledge producer, but truly an artist, who can create works of beauty and pleasure. It saddens me when I hear students tell me that even after they have read an article many times, they still do not understand what the author was trying to say.

We should aspire to write in a way that makes it easy for our readers to grasp what we have to say in as few readings as possible. If they only have to read the article once, we would have saved them a lot of time and energy. They may be more likely to remember us as well. I have written to scholars, thanking them for writing something so clear and well. It makes it easy for me to remember and cite their works.

CHAPTER 21: PERSONALIZING YOUR WORK AND HAVING FUN

I wrote earlier about the writer as artist. If a writer is an artist, then our written works are our masterpieces. Labaree (2012) reiterates, "Academic writing can be and should be a medium for personal expression and artistic creation" (p. 82). Your journal article is your chance to create something of your own, a work of art that has never been seen before.

Have fun with your writing. Use each writing opportunity to leave clues about who you are. For example, I give my participants names that reflect their true personalities. A feisty teacher is given a name reflecting that attribute. A teacher who reminds me of a friend is given that friend's name. I named one participating school after a local (Singaporean) native plant and another after a native monkey to reflect my original training as a biologist. In this way, I imprint my identity on my work, saying, "this work is uniquely mine."

You may think this is rather extravagant or silly, but this is my reward and fun for the hard work I put into writing these pieces.

CHAPTER 22: VALUING AND ENJOYING THE PROCESS, NOT JUST THE OUTCOME

When you begin to see yourself as a writer and then an artist, with academic writing as a means of creative self-expression, you will not experience writing in the same way. You will begin to enjoy the process of creating meaningful works of knowledge and art. As you work on honing your craft, there is something important that I need to tell you. Many works never see the light of day and that is okay. I have written articles that were never published because I did not have the support of my advisors or felt they were not good enough: there is nothing wrong with that. So, do not let failure or a few unpublished or "unsuccessful" works stop you from writing and publishing!

Rejection is part of academic life. We often talk about our successes but rarely our failures; so when you receive your first rejection, you may feel terrible and alone. Do not be disheartened or give up. All academics receive rejection; rejection is the writer's rite of passage. Take whatever feedback has been given to you, make the article stronger, find another journal and send it off again. My third and final article -- what I felt to be my finest piece (and wanted to dedicate to my country for the 50th anniversary of its day of independence) -- was initially called, "Positive and Social Patriotism among Humanities Teachers in Singapore". It was rejected by my first-choice journal, a European journal. The reviewers did not agree with the way I see things.

So I took their feedback and rewrote the article. I gave the article a bit of a twist and decided to focus less on the "positive and social" aspects of patriotism but more on how these ways of understanding patriotism are postmodern instead. Hence, I re-titled my article, "Postmodern patriotism: Teachers' Perceptions of loyalty to Singapore" (Chua & Sim, 2018), and submitted it to an Asian journal, hoping that the editor and reviewers would better understand my perspective, and they did! Of course, my country received a belated anniversary gift three years late, but what did it matter?

The journey towards becoming a better writer has its twists and turns, but stay on the path and keep the faith. Each step you take, even those when it seems you are going the wrong way, all make you a better thinker and writer. As a saying goes in Spanish, "Paso a paso, poco a poco." Step by step, little by little, and before you know it, you would have become a published writer!

* * *

Dear fellow writer, if you have enjoyed reading this book, received value from it in any way or have feedback on how it can be improved, would you be kind enough to leave a review on Amazon? I would greatly appreciate it.

BIBLIOGRAPHY

My reference list acknowledges my intellectual debts and points to good resources to read more about the ideas I have shared here.

Adler, M. J., & Van Doren, C. (2014). *How to read a book: The classic guide to intelligent reading*. New York, NY: Simon and Schuster.

Becker, H. S. (2008). *Writing for social scientists: How to start and finish your thesis, book, or article* (2nd ed.). Chicago, IL: University of Chicago Press.

Brogan, J. A. (1973). *Clear technical writing*. New York, NY: McGraw-Hill.

Chua, S. (2016). Education, culture and the Singapore developmental state: 'World-Soul' lost and regained? By Yeow-Tong Chia. *British Journal of Educational Studies*, *64*(3), 401–403.

Chua, S. (2017a). The ethics of patriotism: A debate by John Kleinig, Simon Keller and Igor Primoratz. *Citizenship Teaching & Learning*, *12*(1), 127–128.

Chua, S. (2017b, August 1). National Education Gets Re-invigorated by Technology. Retrieved May 19, 2019, from the NIE website.

Chua, S., & Sim, J. B.-Y. (2017). Rethinking critical patriotism: A case of constructive patriotism in Social Studies teachers in Singapore. *Asia Pacific Journal of Education*, *37*(1), 1–13.

Chua, S., & Sim, J. B.-Y. (2018). Postmodern patriotism: Teachers' perceptions of loyalty to Singapore. *Asian Education and Development Studies*, *6*(1), 30–43.

Cuba, L. (2002). *A short guide to writing about social science* (4th ed.) New York, NY: Longman.

Devan, J. (2007, October 28). Good writing is not about sticking rigidly to fixed pattern". *The Straits Times*.

Dillard, A. (1990). *The writing life*. New York, NY: Harper Collins.

Elbow, P. (1998). *Writing without teachers*. New York, NY: Oxford University Press.

Gastel, B., & Day, R. A. (2006). *How to write and publish a scientific paper*. Santa Barbara, CA: Greenwood.

Horton, S. R. (1982). *Thinking through writing*. Baltimore, ML: Johns Hopkins University Press.

Krathwohl, D. R. (1994). A Slice of Advice. *Educational Researcher, 23*(1), 29–32, 42

Labaree, D. F. (2012). A sermon on educational research. *International Journal for the Historiography of Education, 2*(1), 74–83.

Lamott, A. (1994). *Bird by bird: Some instructions on writing and life*. New York, NY: Anchor Books.

Masterclass. (2018). Masterclass. Retrieved from https://www.masterclass.com/

Pace, E. (1989, February 7). Barbara Tuchman Dead at 77; A Pulitzer-Winning Historian. *New York Times*.

Palmer, P. J. (1999). *The Active Life: A Spirituality of Work, Creativity, and Caring*. San Francisco, CA: Jossey-Bass.

Pechenik, J. A. (2015). *A short guide to writing about biology* (9th ed.). London: Pearson.

Perry, C. R. (2011). *The fine art of technical writing*. Scotts Valley, CA: CreateSpace Independent Publishing Platform.

Wolcott, H. F. (2009). *Writing up qualitative research* (3rd ed.).

Newcastle upon Tyne: Sage

ACKNOWLEDGMENTS

Thank you, National Institute of Education (NIE), and all the friends I made from 2010 to 2018, while working as a research assistant and associate.

Thank you, Assoc. Prof. Jasmine Sim, for seeing the academic writer in me. You encouraged me to write, co-wrote with me and continued to support me after I left NIE.

Thank you, Mala, for being the best writing buddy one could ask for and being there through all my ups and downs. Thank you for the feedback you have given to me.

Thank you Dr Anneliese Kramer-Dahl for the wonderful academic writing workshops you gave and for the one-on-one sessions where you read and critiqued my work with so much care as if it were your own. You inspire me to be a better writer.

Thank you Carol Rosenblum Perry for connecting with me and giving me incisive feedback about the organization of my book. You have a talent for seeing skeletal misalignments and knowing exactly how to fix them, like a chiropractor of words.

Thank you Daphne H P Ng for your incisive feedback and editorial assistance.

Thank you, Assoc. Prof. Alfredo Bautista for forming the Wednesday graduate group during my time at NIE and having faith in me as a scholar.

Thank you, Rwengabo Rutashoboroka for your compassion and interest in my development as a scholar in my early and most crucial years.

Thank you, Carol Kay, my copyeditor, for a job well done!

Thank you, Ivan, for being excited about my book and wanting me to be successful with it. Thank you for purchasing a print copy and asking me to autograph it. That was the moment I realised I was a 'real' author.

To my many readers who wrote me reviews on Goodreads, Amazon and Facebook. Thank you!

And, thank you to my family – Chua Ee Seng, Choo Soo Kuan and Claire Chua – for the support you've given me in many ways during all the years of my career and even beyond.

ABOUT THE AUTHOR

Shuyi Chua discovered the joy of academic writing while completing her Master's degree in Education in Singapore. From her Master's thesis, she published four journal articles. For updates about the book and more academic writing tips and encouragement, follow her at this page: https://www.facebook.com/GraduateStudentWriter/. You can also check out her other works at https://www.shuyiwrites.com/.